THE
PASSING
OF
THE
TORCH

THE PASSING OF THE TORCH

by

James Chen

The Passing of the Torch
by
James Chen

Copyright by
Destiny Ministries
MCMLXXXVIII

Printed in the
United States of America

Published by
Christian Books Publishing H
Box 3368
Auburn, Maine 04210
207-783-4234

ISBN 0-940232-31-6

Library of Congress Catalog Card Nur   **88-63263**

DEDICATION

To those men and women who sat in a building at 1000 El Embarcadero in an obscure little village called Isla Vista and heard James Chen—weak, broken and infirm — bring these incredible messages.

Lest We Forget

and

To those future generations who will read his words. May you *never* forget and may some of you be found to have been able to carry that torch forward during your lifetime.

and

To the memory of James Chen whose life was so lived as to have left us all a high and holy legacy *and* a debt yet to be paid ... to him and to all those who have come before us who have faithfully carried that torch down to our present age.

and

To those who will carry it forward after we, too, have passed from the pages of history and have joined that great cloud of witnesses who stand there cheering for you who dare to take up where they have left off.

FOREWORD

We plan to keep this book in print for as long as this publishing house exists so it can continue to send forth its challenge and its message to all future generations until Christ comes.

If ever this book goes out of print it is our prayer that someone out there in the distant future will see that it is republished so that its call may never be lost to the people of God.

INTRODUCTION

The Story Behind This Book

This publishing house produces a book entitled *The Torch of the Testimony,* which recounts the history of obscure and often nameless groups of Christians who, throughout church history, have boldly carried the torch of the testimony of the centrality of Jesus Christ.

That particular book brings the history of that torch—and the passing of that torch—up to the late 1800's. But the story did not end there! The torch has been passed on since then. But who is it that has taken the torch? Perhaps many groups have. Many Christians believe it was the Little Flock of China who took up that testimony most faithfully at the point where *The Torch of the Testimony* leaves off. Or was it Bakht Singh of India or Prem

Pradham of Nepal, or someone whom none of us know?

From the years 1930 to about 1950 there was perhaps no greater witness on this earth to the centrality of Christ and His Church than that which was borne by the Little Flock on the mainland China. Or perhaps not. It may take another century to know for certain.

The author of this book was one of the Christian workers in the Little Flock. Just after World War II, Watchman Nee sent James Chen to a little group of believers in Hong Kong. It was there James Chen raised up a large and vital church with a membership numbering in the thousands.

In the 1960's and early 1970's brother Chen and others had to watch as the unity of the Little Flock disintegrated all over Asia. His own church in Hong Kong (like so many others in Asia at that time) went through a horrendous and devastating split.

In 1974 James Chen made a visit to the United States. His health was shattered and, as he predicted (though he was only 62 at the time), he did not have long to live. At the time he arrived in the United States this dear brother felt God was finished with the Little Flock. It was in his heart to see *the torch* passed on to yet another people in another place. He hoped to witness the passing of that torch in his lifetime.

This book contains the messages that expressed that hope. Inside the covers of this book is the challenge he laid before a group of young people in Santa Barbara, California. (Those of us present shall *never* forget that week and those messages.) In speaking to those brothers and sisters, he was speaking, unknowingly, to all future generations concerning the call, the cost, and the way of God in *God's search for a people*—His search for a people, in *every* age, who will bear His testimony during their lifetime. God looks, in every generation, for a people to carry the torch of *His* testimony.

Read this book. Then pass it on to others. Somewhere out there God is now searching for a people through whom He can do a new thing on this earth. Let us hope *this* book find its way into the hands of individuals (and of a people) who have a heart that beats one with His.

Is your heart for His call? Is your heart to seek that torch and burn as a living witness to the centrality of Christ and His Church in all things?

Gene Edwards

These messages were spoken in Chinese through an interpreter to a spellbound audience.

1

HOW GOD FOUND US AND USED US DURING OUR EARLY YEARS IN CHINA

This is the first time I have been in a meeting composed entirely of brothers and sisters who have grown up in the United States and who are also all young people. I am the eldest brother among you, but being here, I feel like I am ten years younger.

A moment ago you heard a little story about my dear friend in Christ, brother Watchman Nee. That story reminds me of the past history of the church in China, and especially the "Little Flock." I seldom speak of myself in public, but this evening I cannot help but mention a few things briefly as I recall past events in China and Hong Kong.

I was brought up in a Christian family, but when I was twenty years old I was not yet saved. I did not even know what being saved meant. At that time I had already studied in a Bible school, but I had no real *life* inside. In 1926 the Lord sent brother Watchman Nee to my school. At first I looked down on him because he did not seem like a strong leader. He was always bending his head, praying. I had never seen anyone like him before. But after he began to preach I realized that his message was different from anything I had heard before because he preached with power. I formed a deep admiration for him after listening to him but once. For ten days there were gospel meetings in which he spoke. It was in those meetings that I was truly saved. I will never forget that period of time in my life. Since then I have had a heart to love the Lord and to seek after Him.

If Watchman Nee were here and if he heard me mentioning his name, he would be very unhappy. I feel I am saying too much about him. He never wanted anyone to exalt Watchman Nee more than Christ. He felt very deeply that his name should never take up even a little bit of the attention due the name of Jesus Christ. The Christians and the churches all over China, although they respected Watchman Nee, seldom mentioned his name—but they exalted Christ. Brother Watchman Nee was not our head, but Jesus Christ was our Head. At that time there was a kind of awareness throughout the churches in China not to respect any person more than Christ.

We Learned to Suffer and to Pray

The Christians in China to whom I refer practiced loving one another at that time. They had a very intimate relationship because they had one heart. This brotherly love brought a very beautiful testimony to China. The Christians paid close attention to the development of their spiritual lives. They learned to hate themselves, to be willing to bear the cross and to suffer in following the Lord.

There were not many Christians like this in China in those days; nonetheless, there were some who were willing to follow the Lord. In nearly every town where we met there were only a few, at first, who gathered together. But because of the abiding of God Himself and the blessing He poured down, by the year 1928 four weeks of special meetings were called in Shanghai.

After those meetings a few brothers went away to a place in the country. They received some light from the Lord and were willing to follow that light, but they did not know how. They shut themselves in a house and prayed together. When they had finished praying, the ground was wet from their tears. These men wanted to follow the love of the Lord. They could not keep themselves from following Him! They realized it would be a difficult way, a hard way. They felt themselves too weak to go on. The only thing they could do was come to the Lord and pray and weep. The love of the Lord is victorious! After prayer, these few people went out. They went village by village to preach the gospel. Not many years afterward—in that area—more than *a hundred* meetings rose up. The people the Lord blessed and used were not educated or special in the world's eyes, but they had an *incomparable love for the Lord.*

Because the churches were under the guidance of the Holy Spirit, and because of the communion of the life we shared, the people in the denominations who observed us all said that we must have had a very strong organization.

But in fact we did not have *any* organization. It was the agreement of the Life by which we lived that brought and held us together. It was the communication of the Spirit. It was the *oneness in love.*

So, you see, the beginning of our story is wonderful.

But the end of our story is very sad.

In the year 1950 the situation in China was changed by the Communists. By that time there were more than 1,000 assemblies throughout the nation. At the beginning of that change, there was still a rapid increase in the number of Christians being saved. Satan hated this very much because he was not winning; consequently, many Christians and many servants of God soon began to undergo serious persecution.

Finally, all the meetings were closed down.

From our point of view this was a great loss, but I believe that God has a wonderful and different point of view about these events. Jesus said, "I will build my church upon this rock and the gates of hell will not conquer her." To us it would seem that the powers of darkness had overcome the church, but we must remember that the word of the Lord is dependable. Hell will never conquer His church. The victory of Satan is only temporary. When Jesus Christ was crucified on the cross, it seemed that the powers of darkness and death had conquered Him, but actually the Lord destroyed them and their ruler *through* His death.

The Lord is the victorious One.

I hope all you brothers and sisters present here tonight are willing to believe the Lord. I hope you are willing to exalt Him and let Him be Head. You seem to join with Joshua—to follow Jehovah with all your hearts. So give the Lord your full attention; follow Him attentively.

We should have a church that can please and satisfy the Lord. No matter how many members there are in the church, if the Lord is not with you—even if you have 2,000 or 3,000 in attendance—it is all useless. It is better that the Lord is with you even if you have only half the number which is here tonight—*if* the Lord abides with you.

He can bless you. He can make your testimony powerful and make this testimony influence the whole nation. You must be a people who actually *love* the Lord. If you are willing to *put up with everything* for Him and His love, then the Lord can use you to give to Him the greatest glory.

I will give you a little illustration of this.

The last time Jesus entered Jerusalem there was a little donkey tied up by the door of someone's house. No one had ever ridden that donkey, but when it was brought to the Lord, He could use it. The donkey was put under the Lord, and used by Him. The Lord was above that little donkey. When this donkey carrying the Lord Jesus Christ entered Jerusalem, the whole city was moved.

Brothers and sisters, if you here in this room have pure hearts to love the Lord, if your devotion toward Him is complete, if you do not seek after your own glory but only seek to exalt Him, if you do not want to achieve anything but only want His will to be done and His plan to be accomplished; if you have such hearts as this, I tell you, the Lord can use you to *finish* His will!

God's Endless Search for a People

There have been more than a thousand years of the testimony of the Lord. Throughout that time the church of the Lord has sometimes gone astray a little from the right way—sometimes quite a little! Each time, when the church needed to come back to the testimony, a group of people was needed to pay certain costs. The Lord has always raised up such a testimony. He did this very thing in my lifetime in China.

But now forty years have passed since our beginning.* We know that forty is the Biblical number of *testing*. Therefore, after forty years, after many people have been tested, the Lord has found that His work in China is not faithful enough. It is not pure enough. Today, all over the Far East the Little Flock is divided. The Little Flock is too far from the way He has chosen.

Now another group of people is needed.

A new people is needed. These people will be required to pay certain costs to return to the original way. May God bless you for this purpose.

You must decide if you are earnest about joining that throng who, in the past, have carried His testimony.

---

*These messages were brought almost exactly 40 years after the birth of the Little Flock in China.

8

You should spend much time praying for the church. At the same time you must read the Bible diligently. The church must be strong in Spirit in order to closely follow the Lord.

May the Lord bless you for His purpose.

Oh, Lord, how happy I am to come to this place to take part in this meeting. I am much consoled to see so many young brothers and sisters with a fervent love for You. May You maintain this beginning love *and not let these young people lose this love as they grow older.* May your love attract them to go on as they should. How much I expect and hope that they will go on this way to eternal glory. Grant grace and strength to every one of them. Bless them abundantly according to their individual needs. Oh, Lord, You are the only hope in the whole earth. Let your name be glorified, your Kingdom come earlier, your will be done on earth as it is in Heaven. Oh Lord, receive our devotion; receive our love for You. We actually love You because You loved us first. Increase our love for You because we confess that our love is not enough. Bless every brother and sister. Hear our prayer. We pray in the Lord Jesus Christ.

2

JESUS CHRIST IS MOVING STRAIGHTLY FORWARD

Who is this who comes from Edom, with garments of flowing colors from Bozrah, this one who is majestic in His apparel, marching in the greatness of His strength? "It is I who speak in righteousness, mighty to save." Isaiah 63:1

This verse speaks about our Lord who is mighty in His strength. Your Lord is going on; He is going forward taking wide steps. God's pace is not slow. He moves forward, whether men do or not.

Whenever they moved, they moved in any of their four directions, without turning as they moved. Ezekiel 1:17

11

This verse describes the wheels of four living beings. Their wheels are going forward in four different directions. God's way of doing things is straight ahead. He never turns back.

"The latter glory of this house will be greater than the former," says the Lord of hosts, "and in this place I shall give peace," declares the Lord of Hosts. Haggai 2:9

When men build houses, they sometimes first build large ones and later build small ones. And sometimes the more building we do, the uglier the structures become. But when God builds, this is never so: the more He builds the greater and more glorious the building becomes.

But He answered them, "My Father is working until now, and I Myself am working." John 5:17

I am finding it very difficult to speak here. Before I came I had prepared something to say, but after I arrived I realized I could not present that message to you. It is because you young people are like a piece of white paper. If I am going to write on this piece of white paper, I must be very careful. If I write the wrong thing, then this piece of white paper is wasted. I think it is better for me to say nothing and to let the Holy

Spirit Himself write upon you. I cannot tell you what you should do or what you should not do. I give way to the Holy Spirit. Let Him speak to you.

I can only tell you some principles by which God does things. From the beginning of time until the appearance of the New Jerusalem, God has *His* own *way. He goes straightly forward.* If you read the Bible carefully, you find out that God never turns back; He only goes forward. In just this way you should follow God. I will give you some examples.

The Ark

The Ark of the testimony left the tabernacle of Israel and fell into the possession of the gentiles. Later it was moved to Kirjath-hearim, and then to the house of Obed-edom, and then to the tent set up by David in Jerusalem. Later The Ark of God's testimony was put into the temple which was built by Solomon. God's testimony moved straightly forward. It never turned back to the tabernacle in Israel. The ark, and the Lord's testimony, went forward.

The work of God became more glorious as time went on. The tabernacle of Israel was built by the Israelites under the leadership of Moses. The glory of God filled that tabernacle. Later,

Solomon built a permanent temple which replaced the tabernacle in the wilderness. The temple was much bigger and more glorious than anything which had been before it. After a period of time, the temple built by Solomon was destroyed by the Babylonians. Seventy years later God allowed the Israelites to return to Jerusalem to restore the temple. When they had hardships and found no way out, God encouraged them through a prophet. He told Israel that the glory of the later temple would be *even greater* than the previous temple.

Each temple was more glorious than the one before. When the New Jerusalem comes, there will be no comparing her glory with all the temples which have come before. The work of God is going straightly forward!

Each work is more glorious than the last.

I told you a little about the work of God in China. I expect that the work of God here will surpass His work in China. If I speak too much about what God has already done, it will appear that I am seeking to lead you back to the past. This we must not do.

I expect you to go forward. Go forward!

This matter of offering yourselves to God for the work which *God* wishes to do is not a matter of trying, of setting up a goal, nor of having some willingness to achieve all these things. We *should* have such a will, but we should also understand *how* God goes forward. We should understand what *God* wants to do today. If we have seen what God is doing today, and if we follow Him, then we can see His glory revealed more and more every day. Always remember what has been on God's heart...at creation, even *before* creation. Seek to find where He is *today* in relationship to that eternal will.

I mentioned some sad things to you which have happened to us. The work on the mainland of China cannot now be seen any more. Unfortunately the nature of the work since that time has changed. The work from the past seems to have dropped from a high peak so that today it's in a lower place.

Let us consider God's way. We know that the number forty in the Scripture is the number of testing. Jesus Christ was tempted in the wilderness for forty days. Moses led the Israelites in the wilderness for forty years. In the Bible the number forty is always the number of testing.

The Lord's work in the Little Flock began

forty years ago. Today I must say the testimony which the Lord raised up in China is going downward. For instance, the golden age of the church in Hong Kong was from 1950 to 1957. From the years 1957 to 1961 the church there did not go up but remained on a horizontal level. Since 1961 it has been going downward. More reecently the testimony there has been greatly damaged. My heart has been greatly hurt. The testimony which God gave us in so many places in China has now also gone down in many places.

In looking at these conditions we are very sad and very disappointed. But it is *not* sad when we return to the Bible. There in its holy record we see how God worked in the past. The work of God always has ups and downs. So whenever you see the *declining* of God's work, you can expect that there will also be an ascending again.

Each peak must be higher than the one before.

For this reason, when I am the most disappointed I am also the most hopeful. I know this: the glory revealed by the *next* work which God will do *must be* greater than the glory of the *last* work which He did.

In the year 1961 when I first heard that the church in Manila (Philippines) had divided, my heart was broken even unto death. This was the first major division ever experienced in the Little Flock. Unfortunately, many more came thereafter. In those days I walked back and forth in my room. I could not sit down and I could not sleep. For so many years we had made the best effort to support this testimony, this work, and its unity; but it was destroyed. Until that time as a people we had been a strong testimony of the unity of the church; but now the church was divided.

What could I say anymore? What I had been hoping, what we expected, was that by means of *this* testimony of the church the plan of God would be accomplished. But now where was our testimony? It was not important that I felt ashamed and could not lift my head among people. That was not important. What was important was that *the will of God* had been destroyed. The plan, the eternal purpose of God, could not go forward. I thought this was simply too great a burden to bear. What should we do? I was very much distressed.

When I was in my greatest hour of suffering I read:

But when the fulness of time came, God sent forth His son, born of woman, born under the Law. Galatians 4:4

This verse, this truth, became my consolation. I had always thought, until I read this verse, that whereas the Israelites should have finished their whole wilderness journey within *two* years, they actually had trouble making it in *forty* years! I had wondered, "Why were the thirty-eight years wasted?"

During the 450 years of the history of the Judges, it seemed that God did not get very far because of the defeats of the Israelites. It had seemed to me that God had not gone forward at that time.

When the Israelites were captives in Babylon for *seventy* years, I had thought this was also a delay of God's will.

But God opened my eyes when I read Galations 4:4. I realized that thirty-eight years had *not* delayed the time of God. Even the 450 years had *not* delayed the accomplishment of God's plan. The seventy years of the Israelites' capture had *not* changed God's schedule either. When *God's* time had *fully* come, He sent His Son. I hope you will all remember this.

In the New Testament there is yet another example that shows us the fulness of time.

... With a view to an administration suitable to the fulness of the times, that is, the summing up of all things in Christ, things in the heavens and things upon the earth. Ephesians 1:10

In the fulness of time things in the heavens and things on earth will be united in Christ to be one. There will be no division. There will only be this oneness in the new heaven and the new earth. Only *one* New Jerusalem, *one* Temple, *one* River of Living Water, *one* Tree of Life, *one* Kingdom, *one* Throne. Everything is *one!*

In the fulness of time the will of God *will* be fully accomplished!

I should not be sad. My sadness is unnecessary. What has happened to us in the Far East is not a defeat. The will of God is going *forward! Straightly forward*! He works continuously. You and I should therefore believe *absolutely!*

So, what is the problem now? The problem is whether *you* can follow the work of God. Will *you* now take part in the accomplishment of His great plan? If you *are* willing to take part in *His* work, that is glorious.

I have seen some possibilities since I have come here among you. I cannot guarantee that things will be done here in a certain way, but I can say that there is a *possibility* for the Lord to work here. My main purpose, my most important purpose, is to see *the work of God* today on the earth.

When I came to you I was told that I was in a new city. A brother told me this place is full of young people. Tonight I am the oldest man present. The meeting here is *new* and the brothers and sisters are *young.* Everything looks new; therefore, I said, "You are a piece of white paper." On this piece of white paper something can be written or drawn which is more beautiful than anything that has been drawn or written in the past.

You have that possibility *if* you are humble, *if* you look intently to the Lord. Give the Holy Spirit freedom. Let the Holy Spirit work freely upon every one of you.

God *can* do a work exceeding all His work in the past. The work which God wants to do now must surpass all that is in the past. Why? Simply because *this* is the principle by which your Lord works.

You should be humble. You should be obedient. You should love Him with all your heart.

All the meetings here, all the service here, should be for only one purpose: to satisfy *Him*! Our *only* oneness is in the accomplishment of *God's plan*. No one should pre-plan anything. We should let the Holy Spirit have His absolute authority here. To all this should be added your urgent and earnest prayer.

I believe deeply that God will do a work here that has never been seen anywhere else. God's glory here will exceed all He has had in the past.

When I hear that God is doing a great and glorious thing here, I will come again! And I will find my place in the back and follow behind you, *to go forward*. You young people can walk fast; I am an aged man and walk slower. I can only follow behind you. But I will still be so happy even if I follow behind. It is sufficient if the Lord can have His glory. May all glory be to Him!

Lord, speak to us. Open and reveal Your will to us. We need You to lead us on. We greatly expect You will do a new thing on this earth. Lord, may You have a new beginning here. If You think we are worthy, may your mercy come upon us. Let us go on together. We look to You. Amen.

3

A NEW WINESKIN
IS NEEDED FOR THE NEW WINE

Since therefore, brethren, we have confidence to enter the holy place by the blood of Jesus, by a new and living way which He inaugurated for us through the veil, that is, His flesh. Hebrews 10:19-20

Therefore we do not lose heart; though our outer man is decaying, yet our inner man is being renewed day by day. II Corinthians 4:16

But no one puts a patch of unshrunk cloth on an old garment; for the patch pulls away from the garment, and a worse tear results. Nor do men put new wine into old wineskins;

otherwise the wineskins burst, and the wine pours out, and the wineskins are ruined; but they put new wine into fresh wineskins, and both are preserved. Matthew 9:16-17

I have shown you how the work of God always moves ahead in a straight path and never turns back, and how each successive work of God becomes more and more glorious. God reveals more and more glory *until the end*! He leads us forward, and His work is always new and living. God never turns back; therefore He never uses an old way. Each time God moves forward, something of His glory is revealed that has *never* been seen before.

Here, then, are principles of God's work: (1) He moves straightly forward, (2) the latter glory is greater than the glory of former times, (3) and a new work lies ahead. I hope that you will remember these three principles.

Ecclesiastes tells us that there is not a new thing under the sun. There is nothing new in the world. Anything happening in the world today will happen again in the future. Indeed, there is really nothing we can call "news" in the world. There are only the old things happening over and over again. Still, according to the principles by which God works, there is never an *old* thing! All that He does is new. Every day there is "news." This is glorious!

We should have new experiences every day. Every day, contact the new things of God. If one day passes in which we are not new enough, our spiritual situation comes to a standstill. I have often confessed my sin to the Lord. It was not that I had done many wrong things; it was only that nothing *new* had happened to me. I had learned no new lesson, and I knew I had failed already. If our life is not renewed day by day, we have a problem before God.

In the same way, if nothing new happens in the church of God, that church has stopped living by God's new life. We can expect that if we are seeing God on earth and among us, we will see Him do new things all the time. He will do things He has never done before. He will do the things He wants done *today*.

We must keep at our praying, asking God to do a new thing in this age. In eternity everything is new. The old world has passed away. There is the appearance of a new heaven and a new earth. Within the new heaven and new earth there is a city called the New Jerusalem. The New

Jerusalem is the bride. In my native toungue the word for a bride is "new woman." So *everything* is new!

This is the work that God wants to do.

You may ask why we need such newness. Only *new men* can enter the new heaven and the new earth. Human beings who have fallen from God have certain ways of thinking. Know this: people want *old* things, not new things! For example, when we go to the museum, the older the pictures, the better. But in the heavens there is no museum. All museums have been burnt away. Museums cannot enter the new heaven and the new earth.

Why doesn't God want old things in a new work of God? Jesus Christ told us it is because the old wineskin cannot contain the new wine. New wine can only be contained in a new wineskin. After the wine is once contained, it is poured out for other men to drink. After a man has drunk this wine he becomes joyous. But when all the wine is drunk up, when there is no wine left, the old wineskin still remains. The wine has gone, but the wineskin is still there.

This is what is meant by an old wineskin. Remember, a wineskin is all that is left when the wine is gone! When wine is gone, what good is the old wineskin?

In every age God always uses a certain group of people. *Those* people are the wineskin. Those people become the wineskin, and the grace of God and Holy Spirit are contained by them. God is the wine, the people of God the wineskin. But after a certain number of years, for one reason or another, God ceases to pour out His grace through a people.

Yet that group of people *is still there.*

It is at this point that this particular group of people becomes the *old* wineskin.

But do not weep. God is at that very moment searching for a new people. He is moving forward!

When God wants to move forward, His wine must be new—and stronger and more abundant than before. If this newer, stronger wine were put into that recently "old" wineskin, the old wineskin would not be able to contain it and would break. Both the wine and the wineskin would be lost! Therefore, for God's work in every age, He longs for—and searches to find—a *new* wineskin.

He *must* find a new wineskin. And when He finds that new wineskin, He will put new wine into it! Be sure, He *will* do it.

The grace of God is always and forever new. God's message is new every morning. The grace that God wants to give the world is forever new, but your Lord needs a new wineskin. Without a new wineskin no new grace can be contained. Without God's grace we cannot deal with the new needs of this particular age in which we live.

One thing is certain: this is the newest age, because it is *now*. And the need of *this* age *exceeds* the need of any of the past ages. The thirsting and hungering of people in this age will require God's *new* grace to satisfy them. God always has new grace. Everyday He has new grace to be given to the world, but there must be a new wineskin to contain it. There must be a new body. *This* is God's need today. I hope that you all see this.

And what is the new wineskin? Please do not misunderstand. Please do not think the new wineskin is a *method* we pick out or invent by ourselves. You know that in Paris, France there are fashion salons which design new styles every day. They want to sell all their latest designs in clothing. Not long after displaying one design, they decide on another new fashion and then they push it. In the church we never need such things. Any new fashion coming from our minds is useless. If it is out of our brain, even the newest plan is old because it comes from the old Adam. It is useless. *God* longs to do a work which no human has ever thought of, a work which He himself has never done before, a work entirely new.

What is this new work? Nobody knows!

When I read the four gospels, I find that Jesus only mentioned the church twice. Only twice. And after He mentioned the church, He never told the disciples how to establish it, how to organize it, or how to promote it. The disciples wanted the church, but they did not know what the church was to be! They had never seen what the church was to be. Jesus Christ only told them, "When the Holy Spirit comes, He will tell you all things. He will lead you into all truth."

Jesus did not foretell these other things to them—what the church is, how to organize the church. If the disciples had known about the church before the coming of the Holy Spirit, they would have gone back and thought it all over.

They would have added something to Jesus' words with their own minds. Then the coming of the church would not have been the real church at all. It would have been men's *ideas* of the church. Jesus never told the disciples what the church should be. He left the secret with the Holy Spirit.

We also find out about the work of the Holy Spirit and the church by means of the epistles written by the Apostles. But as Jesus did not explain everything about the church to the disciples, the Holy Spirit also did not tell us everything through the Apostles. We human beings like regulations, but when we read the Bible we cannot find rules to explain *how* we should establish the church. The Bible tells us a little about how we should meet, but it never tells us how we should start a meeting. We need the Holy Spirit to tell us such things at every moment.

The guidance of the Holy Spirit is always new. This newness is not new ideas worked out in our minds. It is only through the revelation and work of the Holy Spirit that we receive any new thing. Jesus told the disciples they should wait in Jerusalem for the descending of the Holy Spirit.

What the Holy Spirit was like, these men did not know.

If a friend told me to go meet somebody at the airport for him, but did not tell me what that person looked like, what would I do? The disciples were like that. They were waiting for the Holy Spirit, but they did not know at all what He would be like when He descended.

Many people are waiting for the downpouring of the Holy Spirit. They may have a mistaken concept of what is coming; they may have preconceived something. They may have imagined that the downpouring of the Holy Spirit will be just like an electric current. Maybe they have imagined that it is like thunder, but the Lord never said that. Actually, before the Holy Spirit came, nobody knew what He would be like nor what He would do. Thank God for the disciples. When Pentecost came, *then* they knew what the Holy Spirit was. And today, as God seeks a people, when the Holy Spirit comes, only then will we know *what* the new work is, what the new grace is, and not before. A new work of God is done by the Holy Spirit. It is *revealed* by the Holy Spirit.

When the Holy Spirit comes, you will know Him if your heart is really open. You do not need to have any presumption as to what the Holy Spirit is like. The only thing you need is to have a heart willing to wait upon Him.

Do you recall that one day somebody told you that if you believed in Jesus Christ, you could receive His life? What His life was like, you did not know. Before I received Christ, I did not know what "Life" was. You did not know either, thank God; but when we received His Life, you knew, and I knew also! Praise the Lord. It is the same way when the Holy Spirit comes. You know, and I know, and the church knows. Therefore, the new work of God begins by the Holy Spirit. It is done by the Holy Spirit. It is *only* the things which come from the Holy Spirit which are new. Thank God!

The Apostles waited in the upper room in Jerusalem. They waited continuously. And when the Holy Spirit came, what did the Israelites around them say? They said, "These people are filled with *new wine!*" The disciples had become the new wineskin! There was new wine in them. Those who watched them saw that they were new wineskins with new wine in them.

I will say it again: There can be no new work of God on this earth which comes from our brain or our imagination. A new work of God must come from the Holy Spirit. Only the work done by the Holy Spirit is new. If the work is not done by the Holy Spirit, even a "new" method is old.

These are the things we want: new grace, the new work of the Holy Spirit. Only this can meet the need of this age which dawns before you. I believe absolutely that God longs to do a new work. The Holy Spirit still wants to move forward, working continuously. The more He works, the more glorious will be that new work.

This is the work of God. This is the principle of God's work. Let us only hear.

What is our human responsibility?

We have only one responsibility, and *that is to pray.*

I add two more words: *Pray as one heart with one spirit.* There must be a group of people praying together with one heart and one spirit. *All we do is ask God to do a new thing through the Holy Spirit, a new thing through us that has never been done before, a work which we have never seen before and no one has seen before.*

"Oh, God, we ask you to do this work."

I will return to what I said before. You are a very young people. You are a new piece of white paper. It is very possible for *you* to become the new wineskin.

You should pray. You need to pray intensely. You should spend *more* time in prayer. Sometime you need to have fasting prayer because of the responsibility. The burden is on you.

This age is very dark. The Lord will come soon. Before the coming of our Lord the world will be most dark. Out of fear, Satan will be fierce to persecute the children of the Lord who are bearing His testimony at that time. If we have not gained new power, if we have no new grace, no new recognition of Him, If we do not have new experiences, if we have only old things and have become an old wineskin, *how* can we contain the new wine?

Brothers and sisters, we should pray for one thing: "Oh, God, *You* do these things by Yourself. *You* do a new thing."

I hope that you who are in the church here can all say that you have no plans, no picture drawn by anybody. Just put yourselves into the hands of God. Ask God today: "Oh, God, how much more You love the work here than I do. May your will be done. How big a work do You want? We put no limitation upon You. Nobody puts a hand on your work. It is entirely in your hand."

Let the Holy Spirit have absolute authority. Let Him do a new work. Every work of the Lord is different.

We always need the Holy Spirit. On our part, we need prayer: the more, the better. We call the book of Acts the acts of the Holy Spirit. What the Holy Spirit tells us, we may say. But all these things we receive from Him are the result of prayer.

I hope *you* will take up the responsibility for the church and for the work of God. Have more and more prayer asking God to do a *new* work among you. This new work should not be influenced by anybody. No human head should be put upon this work. No human method should be added to this work. We should let the Holy Spirit have absolute freedom. I hope this will happen among you.

If you receive this burden which I now pass on to you, pray for these things. God will hear your prayer. My eyes wait to see such glory. My ears are waiting to hear such news. May your Lord so bless you in these things.

4

LET GOD DECIDE

The Lord Jesus Christ accomplished a great work and, as I have already told you, the work of the Lord keeps going straightly forward. The longer He goes forward, the greater the work. The longer He goes forward, the more glorious the work. Have faith to believe that your God will do newer and greater things. Have faith to believe you will see things that you have never seen before and things you have never even imagined.

When it was time for Jesus Christ to be crucified on the cross, He told the disciples, *"What I have done, you also will do. And you will do greater things than I have done, because I am going to the Father, and the Holy Spirit will descend upon you."*

Now, in order to strengthen your faith to believe such words, let's look at some facts from the Bible.

After His resurrection, Jesus Christ revealed Himself to the disciples during a period of forty days. He told them to wait in Jerusalem for the descending of the Holy Spirit. And though they did not know what the descending of the Holy Spirit would be, they waited. They did not just sit idly about doing nothing, but they prayed. There were 120 people gathered together in Jerusalem praying with one mind.

When I arrived here you told me that the number of brothers and sisters here was around 120. This number is quite close to the number of the disciples and those who were waiting in Jerusalem. There was one thing more about those 120 people: they were very much of one heart. Your situation here is quite similar to theirs because you gather together *joyously*. That proves that there is no hindrance among you, and that there will be no hindrance between you and the Lord. Therefore, only one more thing needs to be added. That is prayer. If you pray intently and continuously, the Lord will do wonderful works.

We all know that during the ten days of

prayer in the upper room, the Apostles never prepared an evangelistic campaign. They did not print gospel tracts and invitation cards to invite people to come to hear Peter. They made no preparations because they did not know what was going to happen. They had no organization, no arrangements. They only did one thing: they prayed.

When the disciples had prayed for ten days, the Holy Spirit came. It was not because the Holy Spirit had come that Peter stood up to preach, but it was because so many converts had heard and seen the Apostle and some did not understand what was happening to them. Peter wanted them to understand. The spectators thought the disciples were drunk. But Peter said, "It is nine o'clock in the morning. We cannot be drunk at this time. It is too early." (What a *practical* response!)

When Peter got up to say this to the throng, it was only to give an explanation about the accusation of being drunk. Almost as an afterthought, he quoted the Old Testament, explaining that what the Israelites were seeing was the coming of the Holy Spirit. Then he rebuked the people saying that they had crucified Jesus Christ. Now Peter had not prepared any of these words. I tell you brothers and sisters, many sermons in Christianity are prepared sermons and many of them are useless. Sermons prepared by men are always from the brain, but Peter's unprepared sermon was moved by the Holy Spirit. His sermon was living, and many people were touched by what he said even though he had no such goal beforehand.

In our preaching of the gospel we have a preconceived idea of how many people we want the Lord to save. Perhaps if the disciples had set up a goal of how many people they wanted to be saved that day, it would possibly have been just thirty to forty people—at the most 300. I believe that they would have never set a goal of 3,000 people. Praise the Lord! They did *not* set a goal beforehand. Their unprepared preaching gave the Holy Spirit the freedom to work! As a result, 3,000 were saved. How wonderful it was! May you see such principles working among you.

Let us see one truth. If we want to see the work of God, we must first believe. We must believe that God is able to do a wonderful work. Then we should pray. And we should pray with one heart without setting up a definite goal. We should believe that God can do a work that is new, wonderful and big...beyond our imagination. If everyone of you receives such a burden, I believe that the Lord will have a new work among you.

The book of Acts lets us see the work of the Holy Spirit; it also lets us see the prayers of the saints. When the Holy Spirit wants to work, we must pray. The more we pray, the more the Holy Spirit will move. When we pray, we prepare a path for the Holy Spirit to work His way.

When the day of Pentecost was over many people had been saved. In the beginning there were 3,000 saved; later the number increased to 5,000. The work was developing far beyond the disciples' imagination. How did they deal with this situation? We all know that later very serious persecution came. How did they deal with such a thing? How do we deal with distresses? By prayer.

With prayer!

When they prayed *with one heart* the earth was shaken. Every one of them was told to bear the testimony for the Lord. Let us realize something: On one side there was the work of the Holy Spirit, but on the other side was the prayer of the saints.

In Acts 10 we again see the effects of prayer.

We all know there was a very strong prejudice among Jewish people against the Gentiles. They would not communicate with the Gentiles. They would not eat with the Gentiles. They looked upon Gentiles as dogs. Therefore, the apostles never had any idea of preaching the gospel to the Gentiles. How could God break through such prejudice and take the gospel to the Gentiles? How? By the same means He used before. On one side it was the work of the Holy Spirit, on the other side it was the prayer of man.

All of Cornelius' family prayed continuously to God. They prayed without ceasing. When the time came, God sent an angel to Cornelius. "Your prayer has been remembered. Your prayer has come to God."

At the same time, God gave Peter the vision of a great cloth with many living things inside it. Some of them were unclean things which Jews could not eat. Then God spoke to Peter, "Come and eat all of them."

After Peter saw this vision and heard God speak, some men came to the house where he was staying. They had been sent from Cornelius. Peter realized that this was an arrangement made by God. He knew he was supposed to go to the Gentiles with the gospel, and he went with his visitors back to Cornelius' house.

Peter had no idea what he was going to do or say at Cornelius' house. He had never prepared a sermon suitable for Gentiles! He asked them, "Why have you asked me to come?" Cornelius told Peter his story, and so Peter stood up to speak. When Peter spoke, he had no idea of repeating the message he had given at Pentecost; but while he was preaching, the Gentiles became converted and did all the things Peter and his companions had done when the Holy Spirit had descended on them. This was something Peter had never expected. Neither could Cornelius and those in his house ever have expected this. This was a *new* work. This new work on one hand was done by the Holy Spirit Himself. On the other hand it was brought about by the earnest prayer of man.

When we desire to see God's work brought in we must pray.

Now let us look at Acts 13. This is the story of the sending of the gospel to places far distant from Jerusalem.

Today there are many movements to preach the gospel in the remote places of the earth. And *today* before any of these movements launch their new operation, people make many plans and preparations of their own. Then they send men out.

In chapter 13 of Acts you will find no such thing. A few prophets and teachers were serving God in fasting and prayer. They came before the Lord. They were moved and touched by the love of the Lord. Their communication with the Lord was so joyous they forgot about eating. They were only attracted by the glory of the Lord. Their prayer turned into *fasting* and prayer.

I tell you again, the brothers in Acts 13 were not expecting any particular thing. These men had not planned anything. Because they had made no preparations of their own, the Holy Spirit was able to speak: "Send me Paul and Barnabas to do the work which I entrust to them." When they heard the Lord's voice, they were of one heart. They put Paul and Barnabas into the hands of the Lord. Paul and Barnabas were sent out. They went many places and the church was raised up in many areas. Many people were saved.

This was a new work. *Here was a work which had never been done before!*

On one hand, it was the guidance of the Holy Spirit. On the other hand, it was the prayer of man. We must be before God and pray until the Holy Spirit speaks among us. We must all be of one heart. We will all recognize, "This is the speaking of the Holy Spirit. This is the will of God. This work will be full of the grace of God and full of the power of God."

Next I will mention something about how the gospel was first brought to Europe. This was also a new work of God.

It is the story of the beginning of the church in Philippi. You all know that before Paul went to Philippi there were several women praying there. They had no building to meet in, but they prayed so much that the place where they prayed became famous as the location for prayer in Philippi. I believe most people in the city did not know what these people were doing when they first began to pray. What was this? A few women were gathered together. I do not know whether they sat or knelt, but what they were doing was praying. Many people went to look at them out of curiosity. What were they doing? Gradually people knew—they were praying.

I am telling you that because of *their* prayer in

that town, a vision was revealed to Paul over in another city, Troas. You can imagine the vision he saw. He saw some people from Philippi requesting him to come and help them. His vision was of the Philippian women praying. Their prayer had become a vision to Paul.

Brothers and sisters, Paul did not go to Philippi because he received a letter of invitation; he did not go because of a telegram. The women in Philippi did not know Paul. They only felt a need. "We need help. We need guidance." They prayed before God. They prayed continuously, and God took the request they offered up to Him and turned it into a vision for Paul.

After seeing this vision, Paul went to Philippi. When he arrived, he did not know where he should begin to preach. He did not know where to start the work, but he heard about something. He heard that by the river there was a group of women who prayed. As I have already mentioned, this group of women had been noticed; their prayer had become famous. When Paul heard that there was a group of women praying, he thought: "I should go and help them. This is my responsibility. There is some possibility that God sent me here for this." Then

Paul went to them and preached to them. Some of them were saved.

Brothers and sisters, the beginning of the church in Philippi was because of prayer. Because of the prayer of man. Because of a group of women who prayed.

(The prayers of sisters are equally as important as the brothers.)

Paul preached the gospel in Philippi and some were saved. But it had all come about because a few women had prayed. Praise the Lord, the church in Philippi later became one of the strongest among the Gentile churches. Why? Because of their prayer.

Paul continued to preach the gospel in Philippi. Soon a girl disturbed by an evil spirit began to hinder his preaching, and Paul drove the spirit away. The master of the girl became very angry and you all know the result. Paul was caught, beaten and put in jail. Paul's body was greatly wounded. He was in chains. He was put in the inner prison.

At midnight he was praying. Then he began singing a hymn. He prayed to the Lord through singing hymns. He prayed, sang hymns, praised the Lord. Suddenly, the earth began to shake and the whole prison began to shake, and the doors of the prison were opened. The chains dropped off all the prisoners. At first while Paul was praying, the prisoners in the jail were very quiet, listening to the praying and singing of Paul and his companion. It was very unusual for those prisoners to be quiet because they were very crude; but while Paul was praying, the Holy Spirit came to control the situation. The hearts of the prisoners quieted down. When the doors of the prison opened and when the chains of the prisoners dropped off, it was quite strange that not one prisoner escaped. This is the dominion of God. That prison became a meeting place.

The man in charge of the prison wanted to commit suicide after the earthquake. But Paul stopped him and spoke to him: "We are all here. No one has escaped." The same evening *that* man was saved. I deeply believe that many prisoners were also saved that night. After they had been set free, I believe they became part of that strong witness of the church in Philippi.

This, then, was the beginning of the church in Philippi. How was it established? Through prayer! Therefore, brothers and sisters, the building up of the church, the power of testimonies, the strong proclamation of the gospel, and the remarkable changes in people's lives are not brought about by any method of man's nor by our thinking.

The most important thing on God's side is the work of the Holy Spirit. On our side, the important thing is prayer.

There is a very heavy burden on my heart. Today the thing we lack the most is real prayer. Many people want to do the work of the Lord. They call meetings for discussions, arguments, planning, preparation and organization. These people are trying to use methods. They use their brains and the most modern ways of our age to promote the Lord's work. How about prayer? There is very little prayer. Very, very little.

Not long ago I went to a meeting of some Chinese people. I asked them when they had their prayer meeting. They said that just two weeks before this meeting they had begun to have prayer meetings. Although they had been meeting together for several years, their meetings for prayer had just begun. I asked them, "How many people were at the prayer meeting— about fifty?" They said, "No." "Forty?" "No." "Thirty?" "No." "Twenty?" "No." "Ten?" They said, "Not yet. We have only nine people who come so far." I was so sad. A church without prayer. How could these people possibly find the work God wants to do on the earth *today*?

Brothers and sisters, I hope that the church here is a church of prayer. If this is a church of prayer, you can bring the blessing from heaven to earth. If you are a church of prayer, you can prepare a path for God by which He can do His work. If you are a church of prayer, you can see the glory of God.

In Christianity today, even though men pray, what they offer as prayer is really not prayer. They use prayer to preach; they use prayer to teach. They forget that prayer is speaking to God and listening to God.

You see, prayer releases our burdens to God. Prayer shows our weakness. Prayer is to ask God to do *His work*. Prayer is the union of our *willingness* and God's *will!*

Brothers and sisters, when God wants to work on the earth, He must have a group of people. God searches for such a people. This people must be in union with His will. The unity of God's will and man's will is brought about through prayer—*this* is the *meaning* of prayer.

I hope that you see something. In the book of Acts, on one hand, there is the work of the Holy Spirit. On the other hand, there is the prayer of man. The two things come together and we see the glory of God.

So we should pray. One other thing. We should also *believe*. Absolutely believe. We must be willing to lay down all methods. We may not depend upon our effort or our wisdom, but we must depend solely upon prayer. This requires very great faith.

May God bless us. The grace of God, the power of God, the glory of God, the work of God are all waiting to be revealed, but first our prayers are necessary. If we put on prayer, the glory of God will be manifested.

5

GOD'S NEED OF MAN

*For the Son of Man has come to seek and to save that which was lost.*Luke 19:10

*But an hour is coming, and now is, when the true worshipers shall worship the Father in Spirit and truth; for such people the Father seeks to be His worshipers.*John 4:23

*And He said to them, "Follow Me, and I will make you fishers of men."*Matthew 4:19

One very wonderful and glorious fact about God is that He needs man!

Whenever God wants to start a work on the earth, He must first gain a group of people. Another wonderful thing about God is that His various works upon this earth, in their appearance, are always different. We cannot do God's work according to past traditions, past patterns or past customs. The appearance of God's work is always new, but the fundamental principle of God's work never changes because God is an unchanging God.

Why did God wish to create man?

One very simple answer is that God *needs* man. There has never been a factory that produced goods which people did not need. The products from the factory must be needed. It is the same way with God and man. God wants and needs whatever He created.

Why does God want to save man?

Because if the Lord does not regain this fallen man, there will be no fulfillment of His need. The salvation of man is partly for God's own need. The Lord Jesus said, "The Son of Man came to seek and to save the lost." Why did He come to seek and save lost men? He came because of His own nature, which is love. He loved man, therefore He had to save man. But more than that, He came to fulfill His plan. In His plan there is a basic *need* for man. If there is no man, God's plan cannot be accomplished.

And why must your Lord have man before He can accomplish His plan on earth?

The answer to that question is glorious. We should know that when God created the earth He was preparing a dwelling place for man. This very planet, earth, has been given to *us!* Since God has given us this earth, whenever He wants to do something here, He must have our agreement. For instance, perhaps I built a house and gave it to brother Gene to live in. Later, if I wanted to enter that house, I would first have to have Gene's agreement. It would then be his house, and if I entered it without his agreement, I would be doing something against my principles. God is like this. He has principles which are part of His very nature. He cannot do something against Himself. Since God has given this earth to man, whenever your Lord wants to work here on this planet He must have man's agreement. The will of man must agree with the will of God!

Incredible, is it not?

Remember what was said in chapter one of Genesis? When God created man, He created him in His own image. Why should He create man in His image and likeness? Simply because God wants us to represent Him. Why should we represent Him? Because God wants us to manage the whole of this planet. He wants us to manage the birds in the sky, the fish in the water, and the beasts on the earth.

You know that every nation has commanders of the air force, of the army and of the navy, but such men are only commanders of *branches* of the military. *We* are the chief commander of all living things upon this earth. The Word of God says that God wants to have the generations of man to govern this whole earth. God not only prepared this earth for us to live on, but He also handed this planet over to us to manage.

A Chinese poet, when he looked up into the sky one night, wrote, "How great the universe is. Oh, how small man is; we are small like eggs." But God did not intend it to be that way. He gave great power to man to manage this whole world. The power given to man exceeded that given to angels.

I used to think that if I could be like the angels I would be satisfied. Now I do not feel that way. Even if God wanted me to be an angel, I would not want to be one. I want to be a man! I do not want to be an angel because men are higher than angels—much, much higher. I am a man.

Brothers and sisters, I hope every one of you will be proud that you are a human being. We are *men*, hallelujah!

At a certain time God himself became a *man*. The Son of God did not want to be an angel. The Son of God came here to be a man. Think how glorious this is. The plan of God is to be accomplished by a man. Because God has put this earth in our hands for management, He cannot do anything here on earth by Himself.

Do you remember the story told in Genesis 2? God brought all the living things before Adam and whatever Adam named them, those were their names. You can imagine that to name a tiger was not easy. Why did not God name the tiger all by Himself? Because He had already put these living things under Adam's management. Therefore, when God wanted to give names to the living things, He had to give Adam the job. Their wills had to agree. Whenever God wants to do something on this earth, He must have the willingness and agreement of human beings.

Here we find the principle for prayer. Why should we pray? After all, God knows everything. Before we pray He knows our need, and He is full of love. He will provide us with what we need. Why must we pray before God will give? God has the power to do His work by Himself. He can work. Why does He wait until we pray?

The Bible tells us that whatever we bind on earth, He will bind in heaven. Whatever we set free on earth, He will set free in heaven. The setting free in heaven is based on the setting free on earth. If the earth does not bind something, then God will not do the same in heaven. Why? Heaven is limited by the earth. Why? Because God has put this earth in the hands of man. If we want God to do something on the earth, then there must be our willingness, our agreement with God.

The meaning of prayer is that we say to God, " I want; I am willing; I agree; I will do." God can do something on this earth when we have such a willingness before Him. This is the principle of prayer.

Brothers and sisters, this is the principle of God's work. You can see these principles clearly in the Bible. Let us look again at the Old Testament. You recall that the Israelites were persecuted by Pharaoh in Egypt. There was much suffering. Their yearning had come before

God in heaven. But God did *nothing*. Do you think God was cruel, that He had a lack of love? Was He not willing to save them? Why did God wait 400 years?

Because God could not find the right man. He did not have a man who understood His will. He did not have a group of people for Himself. There was not a group of people on this earth standing for God's will until He raised up the man Moses. Then with Moses came Aaron and Joshua. They saw the will of God, and then they stood for God's will. They said "Amen" to God's will. Therefore, God could begin to work among the Israelites, and He saved them out of Egypt.

Before God begins His work He must have a group of people. There were 450 years in the period of the judges of Israel in which there was no king. Everyone did what he himself thought was good. God did not want the Israelites to go on in such a situation. God wanted to establish the kingdom of Israel, but He had no people. He did not begin to do a glorious work among the Israelites until He gained Samuel and David and all the followers of David. *Then* the kingdom of Israel was established.

Now we come to the New Testament. Before Jesus Christ was born there were two people who prayed continually. One was a brother and one a sister. They lived in the temple, praying without ceasing. (Consider that!) When God sent His Son to earth, there was somebody on earth *asking* Him to send His Son. Their prayer was, "If your Son has not come, I cannot die. If your Son has not come, I cannot leave this world. I must wait until your Son comes, then I can leave this world peacefully." What was the result? The Son of God came!

Throughout the Bible, each time God's work was accomplished there was a people standing for God's will on earth and praying for His will.

Today, God is searching for such a people!

Lord, your will should be done on earth. Your plan should be accomplished. Your kingdom must come. Your name should be exalted all over this land. You should have glory on this earth. Your church should be built upon the earth. We say "yes" to your will. We say "no" to anything else. We agree with you and we receive your plan.

What a prayer!

There must be people who pray this way, people who stand for God's will. Can God have such people? If He does, then He can work in this age. This is a fundamental principle of God's work, and it is very glorious.

God could do things by Himself; certainly His power is great enough. His wisdom is able to conquer all difficulties; His abundance is great enough to cover all things. On the basis of His great power alone, He does not need us. But God wants us to be His co-workers. God wants you and me to have a part in *His* plan. God wants us to have a part in His work. God has reserved for us the opportunity to live for Him.

The Bible tells us that if we suffer with Him, we shall have glory with Him. But do not imagine that the glory we will share with Him is that someday we will sit on the throne with Him. No! We should see that *right now* we have a portion in the accomplishment of God's great plan. *This* is the glory that we share with Him!

If a great building is constructed and if I have taken part in designing that building, I have labored for that building. I have an investment, a portion, in that building. That is my glory. Just think, you and I have a portion in God's building. God's greatest building, the most glorious building ever. How wonderful!

Brothers and sisters, you can now see that there is a great need right now ...here...today. You must put yourselves in the will of God. *Live on this earth for the will of God.* We live on the earth for the plan of God, the eternal work of God. This is the meaning of our lives. Our salvation is meaningless if we spend our lives on breathing, eating, and dressing.

You were saved, you *are* saved for the eternal will of God.

God needs a group of people who will follow His will. God wants to have such a people. They are too few. Such people are difficult to find. Therefore, Jesus came to *seek* them. He wanted to come and look. He asked, "Who is willing to fill God's request? Who is willing to say 'yes' to God's plan?"

God is *still* seeking; He wants to have such a people. Today He is in search of such a people.

I say again, God needs man. The plan of God needs man. Whenever God wants to begin His work or to do something on earth, He needs man. God needs a group of people who can say an absolute "Yes!" to His will.

See this glorious calling!

I hope the brothers and sisters here will see this and will answer God's request.

6

A HEART FOR GOD'S WILL

But now your Kingdom shall not endure. The Lord has sought out for Himself a man after His own heart, and the Lord has appointed him as ruler over His people because you have not kept what the Lord commanded you. Samuel 13:14

But the Lord said to him, "Go, for he is a chosen instrument of mine, to hear My name before the Gentiles and kings and the sons of Israel; for I will show him how much he must suffer for My name's sake. Acts 9:15-16.

I have talked about how God seeks for men who have pure, true hearts toward Him. Having a pure, true heart for God is fundamental if you want to receive the mercy of God. I believe that when a person is first saved, his heart is always pure. I believe that you brothers and sisters sitting here all have hearts that are pure and true before the Lord.

We have to ask the Lord to *keep* our hearts this way. If it is not the Lord Himself who keeps our hearts, it is very easy for us to become impure.

No one should have the confidence in himself that he will not change, but if we truly do not trust ourselves and if we put our hearts into His hands, He will keep us pure before Him forever. But having true hearts is not enough.

We are not necessarily after God's own heart when we seek Him and His blessing. A person may have a true heart for God without being after God's own heart. If we let God do a great deal of work in us, then we can become people after *His own heart.*

The scripture we read this evening speaks of God's desire for a people who are after His heart. I Samuel 13:14 was spoken to King Saul. The Lord said, "Your kingdom shall not endure. I have sought a man who is after *My* heart." The Lord was pointing to King David. Saul's heart did not match God's heart. His kingdom could endure no longer. Saul's value to the Lord soon ended. King David was a person after God's own heart, and *His* kingdom is forever and ever.

Here we see two types of vessels. One vessel is just of *temporary* use. It will be set aside like a paper cup or plate—after one use it is thrown away. Of course, a plastic plate is useful, but its usefulness *does not last long*. In my home there are some expensive vessels. Some of them have been passed from generation to generation. Some have been passed down for several hundreds or even thousands of years. These are durable vessels which can be used for a long time. Brothers and sisters, what kind of vessels do you want to be—*temporary* vessels, or vessels which can be *used by God* for a long, *long* time? I believe that you all want to be vessels used forever by God.

In my lifetime I have seen a large number of people who have been chosen by God. Some are only used by God once or twice and then are put aside. Some lose their function after just a couple of years. Have they truly been used by the Lord? Yes! God has used those people, but unfortunately He was only able to use them *temporarily*.

I expect you brothers and sisters to devote

yourselves to God with true hearts, to love the Lord and to pray sincerely, saying:

"Lord, I love You. I seek your glory; I look after your ways; I only seek for your will to be done. I love You with my whole heart, my whole soul. I have no other hope on earth except in You. I devote all my strength to You. For any use I may be to You, I am yours."

But, brothers and sisters, we not only need sincere hearts, we need one more prayer:

"Lord, I put myself in your hands. Please do your work in me according to your will. May your work be done in me to make me a vessel after your heart. And may your work be done in me to make me a person who seeks your need."

There is a hymn in China that expresses this very thought: "Lord, I put myself in your hands. I believe You are willing to bless me and give me grace. Break me like the five loaves of bread which were put in your hands. Oh, Lord, break me. Do not mind my pain. Work on me until I can be used for your will. Then 5,000 people will be fed."

Brothers and sisters, we should put ourselves wholly in His hands.

Now let us continue the story of Saul and David. When Samuel spoke to King Saul, David was still very young. He was tending the sheep in the wilderness. No one in Israel noticed David. But the eyes of Jehovah searched the face of the whole earth. He missed no one. He did not forget one person. He did not overlook anyone. Whose heart was true toward Him? What man had let the Lord work in him to the point that he could fit God's will?

At the time the Israelites forced Samuel to anoint a king for them, Samuel could not find one person who was after the Lord's heart. Samuel had to choose someone from among the Israelites who could, comparatively, have been said to be a king. King Saul was one head taller than other men. Comparatively, he was the tallest. Saul was not chosen to be the king of Israel because he was after the heart of God; he was chosen because comparatively he looked the most like a king. God had not done any work in Saul yet. It was not that God had not wanted to work in Saul, but Saul had never put himself unconditionally in God's hands to allow God to work in him.

This was not so of David. David was a person who put himself entirely in the hands of God. Therefore, God could do His best work in David.

Look at David's family. He had eight brothers, of whom he was the youngest. According to Chinese custom, the youngest son is always the most loved by his parents. It was not so with David; his parents treated him poorly. David received the least love. He was sent to the wilderness to take care of the family's flock. He had no chance to study. He received no protection from his parents and no assistance from his brothers and sisters. By going into the wilderness, he lost all his friends.

David took care of the sheep and was very lonely. This was painful, and a great suffering for such a young man. So David turned to the Lord in his suffering and wrote Psalms saying, "My parents forsake me but Jehovah receives me."

You see, the environment in which there is *most suffering* always produces the *most useful men.* God was even willing to let David suffer to carry on His work in him.

Brothers and sisters, do you think you have difficulties in your present circumstances? Are you disappointed, sad? If you have seen the wonderful will of God, You will praise the Lord for what you are going through. While in the middle of the worst circumstances, it is true that you must learn many lessons from God.

If we do not learn, we suffer in vain.

The Bible says that our Lord learned to be obedient through His suffering. Coming into distresses and suffering is one thing, but *learning* to be *obedient* while suffering is yet another. I am not asking you how much you have suffered. I am asking you, "How many lessons have you learned and how much obedience have you learned when you suffered?

Let us see what kind of lessons David learned from his hardships.

First, David learned to come nearer to God. In his loneliness he learned to enjoy the abiding presence of God. David suffered a lot, but he had no one to tell—except God. David learned to *pray*. David came closer and closer to God through prayer. And anyone who keeps praying gradually learns another lesson—that of *praising*.

God became David's consolation and his joy. Then he began to praise God. When David was praising God, he naturally wrote a lot of hymns.

He played his harp and praised the Lord. His music was the highest expression of his closeness to God. There was the prayer, the praise, the singing, and the music for his spirit to God. (When Saul was distressed and David played the harp for him, Saul was relieved.) Even David's playing of the harp was full of the power of the Spirit.

We all know that it was dangerous for David to take care of the flock in the wilderness. There were always lions, bears, and wolves there which wanted to kill and eat the sheep. It was David's responsibility to protect the sheep. He had to drive the beasts away, but he was just a boy. David had to learn another lesson. Just how could David deal with such a difficult situation? How could a young boy protect the sheep? It was during this time that David learned to depend upon God. He had no one else to depend upon. He learned to kill the attacking beasts with stones.

I believe that he must have practiced throwing stones every day. Whenever he had time, he practiced. Then when the bears and wolves came, with just one throw David could kill them. If he was not able to hit his target exactly, not only would the sheep be lost, but he would even lose his own life. He kept practicing. Because of this, David became a young man who could even conquer the hero of an opposing army.

Every great victory is achieved by first winning many small victories. If we cannot conquer small temptations and small attacks, how can we conquer the great enemy? It was in the wilderness that David experienced his first victories.

When you are undergoing a trial, you may begin to grumble against God, but after you have learned the lesson and have become a useful vessel, then you will thank your Lord for giving you such trials.

I thank God always that He has given me a lot of trials in the past. *If today I am a little useful in the hands of God, it is because of what I have learned in my times of distress.*

Do you want to be a people after the heart of God? Then you must put yourselves into the hands of God. Let *Him* prepare your environment and all your circumstances. Let Him continually do His work in you. Then you can become a person after His heart.

When David was in the wilderness, he was

continually learning lessons from the Lord. No one else was paying any attention to him. *His* own parents looked down upon him. In fact when Samuel was looking for the one to be anointed king among his brothers, the only one who was not called upon was David. His parents thought that God absolutely would not select David to be the king. But a person who is looked down upon by men may one day be the very one who is selected by God.

Do no be afraid to be unknown, unrecognized. Do not be afraid that no one will pay attention to you. God will ask, "Has this person come to the place that he is after My heart?" *God will never forget you.* God will not leave you. When the time comes, He will announce, "I have found someone. Here is a person after my own heart." At that time you will become a useful vessel.

Today God is looking for this type of person.

You brothers are not living in a big city in America. It would seem that if you wanted to be well known, you would need to move to New York. Brothers and sisters, God will never overlook you. The only important thing to Him is whether you are after His heart. You are living in a very remote place—an almost unknown place.* That does not matter; God will pick you up and put you in the most important place— where you are needed in His Kingdom. He will use you greatly.

God is looking for men who are after His heart. I believe you who are sitting here can all become people who are after the heart of God. I am a person of little faith; I will be fully satisfied if *one half* of you who are here *become people after God's heart.*

In David's day how many men were found to be after God's heart? *Only one.*

Why are diamonds so expensive? Because there are so few of them. Ordinary stones are of no value because there are so many; anyone can pick them up. The fewer there are of a certain thing, the more valuable they become. This is why it is so glorious to find a person who is after the heart of God. I hope that *you will* have this glory.

Now we come to another vessel. God sent Ananias to lay hands on Saul of Tarsus, who would become Paul. In the beginning, Ananias

Isla Vista had a population of 16,000.

rejected the Lord's instructions, saying, "He is the man persecuting the church!" But the Lord told Ananias, "He is my chosen instrument."

What is a chosen instrument? Men have many useful instruments, but only one that is chosen to meet a certain need. For instance, when you go to the department store to purchase a tool, you find many which are alike. You must make a choice. You want to pick out the finest tool to use for your work. Then you can say, "This is my *chosen* instrument. This is the one I have chosen from among thousands and thousands. It is the most useful."

This is what the Lord did with Paul. Today he is searching for such a man and for such a people. *Chosen.* Chosen instruments for *His* work.

"Here is My chosen instrument. Not only does he have a true heart toward me, not only is he usable for my purposes, not only is he after my heart, but he is also the most valuable instrument I have."

Paul once said, "I consider myself not in the least inferior to the most eminent Apostles." On the other hand, he said that he had known more suffering than anyone else. No Apostle suffered more than Paul. He was a most useful instrument in the hands of God. He had received the greatest, the highest, revelation from God. He had heard a deep and hidden word. He received and enjoyed the greatest abundance from God, and he suffered greatly.

The Lord's work in Paul not only influenced the whole of Asia Minor, but the whole of Europe and the area around the Mediterranean Sea. Paul's epistles to the church have given it the most enlightenment and revelation from God. The church has received the greatest assistance from Paul's writings. Paul was actually an instrument chosen by God to be the most useful, the most important instrument He had. Why could Paul be such an instrument?

First of all, he was courageous because he had been saved by God's grace. Secondly, he matched the Lord. He pushed the whole world aside because he matched Christ. The only thing Paul wanted was Christ. He was not after evangelism, nor a movement, nor numbers, nor fame. He was after Christ.

Paul also had much opposition. Whenever his life was in danger, he was unafraid. He knew that when he went to Jerusalem there would be danger and chains waiting for him, but he did not care. He said, "Even if I die in Jerusalem, I am willing." *For the will of God, he did not value his life.* His life had been sacrificed. He could not oppose God's will.

In every situation, this great church planter was unafraid of the difficulties and dangers. Because Paul cared for his own life *less than any man in the world did,* he became an instrument greatly used by God.

Brothers and sisters, I do not have many days left on this earth. I am hopeless. I am hopeless because I am physically weak. My only hope is that I may become an instrument for His use. I will be satisfied even if I become a small cup. On the other hand, you have a very great future because you are young. You are physically strong and you have long days ahead. You have a lot of opportunities to let God do His work in you. If you are willing to be useful instruments, God can do *His* work in you and His eternal purpose through you.

This is my expectation for you.

Please remember always, though, the kind of people whom God seeks in this age. I expect that many people here can be useful instruments, greatly used by God to influence all America and the world. To hasten God's Kingdom on earth we must be very willing to let God's plan, God's will, be done on this earth.

May God put this will into all of your hearts.

After you have read this book, you will want to read *The Torch of the Testimony,* by John W. Kennedy, which recounts the incredible story of those groups from 360 A.D. until 1900 A.D. who have gallantly, gloriously and faithfully carried high that sacred, blood-stained torch of *His* testimony.

During the lifetime in which *you* live, may your Lord search for—and find—a people through whom can come a *new work of God.*

BOOKS by Gene Edwards

DIVINE ROMANCE

"How can I go about loving the Lord personally, intimately?" No book ever written will help more in answering this question for you. Not quite allegory, not quite parable, here is the most beautiful story on the love of God you have ever read. Beginning in eternity past, you will see your Lord unfold the only purpose for which He created all things. Plunging into time and space, you behold a breathtaking saga as He pursues His purpose, to have a bride! See His love story through His eyes. Be present at the crucifixion and resurrection as viewed from the heavenly realms. You will read the most glorious and powerful rendition of the crucifixion and resurrection ever described. The story reaches its climax at the end of the ages in a heart-stopping scene of the Lord at last taking His bride unto Himself. When you have finished this book, you will know the centrality of His love for you. A book that can set a flame in your heart to pour out your love upon Him.

A TALE OF THREE KINGS

A book beloved around the world. A dramatically told tale of Saul, David and

Absalom, on the subject of brokenness. A book used in the healing of the lives of many Christians who have been devastated by church splits and by injuries suffered at the hands of other Christians.

OUR MISSION

A group of Christian young men in their early twenties met together for a weekend retreat to hear Gene Edwards speak. Unknown to them, they were about to pass through a catastrophic split. These messages were delivered to prepare those young men spiritually for the inevitable disaster facing them. Edwards presents the standard of the first century believers and how those believers walked when passing through similar crises. A remarkable statement on how a Christian is to conduct himself in times of strife, division and crisis. A book every Christian, every minister, every worker will need at one time or another in his life.

THE INWARD JOURNEY

A study in transformation, taking the reader through a journey from time's end to grasp the ways of God in suffering and the cross, and to bring an understanding to why He works the way He does.

LETTERS TO A DEVASTATED CHRISTIAN

Edwards writes a series of letters to a Christian devastated by the authoritarian movement, who has found himself on the edge of bitterness.

PREVENTING A CHURCH SPLIT

This is a study in the anatomy of church splits, what causes them, their root causes, the results, and how to prevent them. A book every Christian will need someday. This book could save your spiritual life, and perhaps that of your fellowship.

CHURCH HISTORY:

These two books bring to bear a whole new perspective on church life.

REVOLUTION, THE STORY OF THE EARLY CHURCH, Vol. 1

This book tells, in a "you are there" approach, what it was like to be a Christian in the first century church, recounting the events from Pentecost to Antioch. By Gene Edwards.

THE TORCH OF THE TESTIMONY

John W. Kennedy tells the little known, almost forgotten, story of evangelical Christians during the dark ages.

BOOKS By Jeanne Guyon

EXPERIENCING THE DEPTHS OF JESUS CHRIST

Guyon's first and best known book. One of the most influential pieces of Christian literature ever penned on the deeper Christian life. Among the multitudes of people who have read this book and urged others to read it are: John Wesley, Adoniram Judson, Watchman Nee, Jesse Penn-Lewis, Zinzendorf, and the Quakers. A timeless piece of literature that has been on the "must read" list of Christians for 300 years.

FINAL STEPS IN CHRISTIAN MATURITY

This book could well be called volume two of **Experiencing The Depths of Jesus Christ.** Here is a look at the experiences a more advanced and faithful Christian might encounter in his/her walk with the Lord. Without question, next to **Experiencing The Depths,** here is Mme. Jeanne Guyon's best book.

UNION WITH GOD

Written as a companion book to Experiencing The Depths of Jesus Christ, and includes 22 of her poems.

GENESIS
SONG OF SONGS
Jeanne Guyon wrote a commentary on the Bible; here are two of those books. *SONG OF SONGS* has been popular through the centuries and has greatly influenced several other well-known commentaries on the Song of Songs.

THE SPIRITUAL LETTERS OF MADAME GUYON
Here is spiritual counseling at its very best. There is a Christ-centeredness to Jeanne Guyon's counsel that is rarely, if ever, seen in Christian literature.

THE WAY OUT
A spiritual study of Exodus as seen from "the interior way."

THE BOOK OF JOB
Guyon looks at the life off Job from the view of the deeper Christian life.

CHRIST OUR REVELATION
A profound and spiritual look at the book of Revelation.

OTHER BOOKS BY CHRISTIAN BOOKS

TURKEYS AND EAGLES, by Peter Lord

Hagen and Selin have been abandoned by their parents. But they have been adopted by a flock of turkeys. Are they eagles? Or are they turkeys? Or is it possible they are eagles that have been turkeyized? But even more important, is it possible that the greatest of all tragedies has befallen you? Are you an eagle that has been turkeyized, an eagle that doesn't even know he is an eagle?

This book could very well transform your life, for it has profoundly affected the thousands of Christians who have heard Peter Lord tell the story.

In the finest tradition of Christian story telling, which dates back all the way to the Lord's parables, this masterfully told tale contains the very heart of the gospel as it pertains to living the Christian life.

AUTOBIOGRAPHY OF JESUS CHRIST

Matthew, Mark, Luke and John are blended together into one complete story of the life of Jesus Christ told in the first person. It is as though you are reading the diary of the Lord Jesus Christ.

A unique and wonderful devotional tool and a totally new discovery of the greatest story ever told, the greatest life ever lived.

(Conferences on the deeper Christian Life are held annually through the United States. Write for further information.)

The following prices are for the year 1988 only; please write for our catalog for price updates and for new releases. All books are paperback unless otherwise noted.

Turkeys & Eagles (Peter Lord)	$ 9.95
Autobiography of Jesus Christ (hb)	$ 9.95
on cassette tape (6 tape set in album)	$29.95
Preventing a Church Split (Edwards) (hb)	$ 9.95
A Tale of Three Kings (Edwards)	$ 6.95
The Divine Romance (Edwards) ($10.95 hb)	$ 7.95
Experiencing the Depths of Jesus Christ (Guyon)	$ 6.95
The Inward Journey (Edwards)	$ 7.95
Letters to a Devastated Christian (Edwards)	$ 4.95
Our Mission (Edwards)	$ 7.95
Revolution, Vol. 1 (Edwards)	$ 6.95
Practicing His Presence (Lawrence, Laubach)	$ 6.95
Union with God (Guyon)	$ 6.95
Final Steps in Christian Maturity (Guyon)	$ 6.95
The Spiritual Guide (Molinos)	$ 6.95
Torch of the Testimony (Kennedy)	$ 7.95
Mme. Guyon's Letters	$ 6.95
Fenelon's Letters	$ 6.95
Guyon's Commentaries:	
Genesis	$ 6.95
Exodus (The Way Out)	$ 6.95
Song of Songs	$ 6.95
Job	$ 7.95
Revelation (Christ, Our Revelation)	$ 7.95
The Passing of the Torch (Chen)	$ 6.95
When the Church Was Young (Loosley)	$ 7.95

Christian Books Publishing House
The Seedsowers
P.O. Box 3368
Auburn, Maine 04210
207-783-4234
Visa-MasterCard accepted

These books are available through your local Christian book store.